Our Family Genealogy:
the Austin Family
Book One

Wanda Austin Nelson

Disclaimer:

This book is intended only for family history preservation. The author is not claiming any of this research to be solely her own. It is not intended to be for any historical documentation. It is only for preserving family records. Neither the author nor the publisher shall be held liable or responsible to any person or entity, directly or indirectly, for any information in this book. All the information therein has been documented by other researchers, including the Austin Family Association of America. This book is to be used for general genealogy research, and to help record the data that many people, including the author, have put together through long years of research. The author does not intend to infringe upon any of the work of others: this book is intended only to be a written record.

Credits:

> Austin Family Association of America, along with their excellent   researchers

> All of the Austin family researchers, past and present, who have ever helped the author, or anyone, in any way

Chapter One

The name Austin is one to be proud of. We are related to Kings, Military leaders, Poets, Inventors, Musicians and American Indians.

The Biblical name Augustus is Latin in origin and its meaning is majestic or venerable. Augustus was the title of the first Roman emperor Caius Julius Caesar Octavianus. It was during the reign of Augustus, that Jesus Christ was born.

Augustine of Hippo November 13, 354 – August 28, 430), also known as Augustine, St. Augustine, St. Austin, St. Augoustinos, St. Augustin, Blessed Augustine, or St. Augustine the Blessed, was Bishop of Hippo Regius (present-day Annaba, Algeria).

He was a Latin philosopher and theologian from the Africa Province of the Roman Empire and is generally considered as one of the greatest Christian thinkers of all times. His writings were very influential in the development of Western Christianity. (Wikipedia)

Our story begins many years ago..... in the country of England, about 1340. Henry I Aysten Austin was born there, as far as anyone can tell.

Without him, none of our family would be here today.

He lived in Horsmonden, Kent, England, a village in Kent, on the Weald.

It is situated on a road leading from Maidstone to Lamberhurst, three miles north of the latter place. The village church, St Margarets, is located some miles away from the center toward Goudhurst.

Henry became a father, in 1374, to a son, Henry II Aysten Austin, named for his father.

He was born in Horsmonden, Tonbridge, Kent, England. Henry II married a woman named Susanna, from Surrey, England.

Henry II Aysten Austin died in 1450, at Benenden, Kent, England. He was seventy-six years old.

Henry and Susanna's sons were: Henry III Austen (born 1400), Richard I Aysten Austin (born 1402), Thomas Austen (born 1404), John Austen (born 1406) and Stephen Austen (born 1408).

Richard I Aysten Austin was born in Brenenden, Kent, England, and lived there for his entire life. He married a woman named Johane, and they both died in the year 1443.

Their sons were: John Austen (born 1420 in Wingham, Kent, England) and Richard II Aysten Austin (born 1428).

Richard II Aysten Austin married a woman named Godlive. They had two sons, and Richard died sometime after 1458 in Yalding, Kent, England.

His sons were: Richard III Aysten Austin (born 1454) and William Aysten Austin (born 1458).

William Aysten Austin continued our line. He married Elizabeth, and they had a son in 1484, in Yalding, Kent, England (where William died in 1522). Their son was Stephen Aysten Awstyne Austin.

Stephen married twice.

His first wife was Dorothy Packham and they one son, Robert Aysten Austen(born about 1512). Robert was the ancestor of the English novelist, Jane Austen.

Stephen re-married a woman named Margaret and they had five children: William Austen (born 1516), John Stephen Austen (1520), Mary Austen (1526), Susan Austen(1528), and Thomas Henry Austen (1533). William was the forefather of Stephen Fuller Austin, the Father of Texas. Stephen Aysten Awstyne Austin died in 1532, at Staplehurst, Kent, England.

John Stephen Austen was the forefather of our particular line. He married Margaret Wrigley. They had two sons: Richard Austen (1544) and Roger Austen(1546).

John Stephen Austen died at Staplehurst, Kent, England, in 1557, his wife having died in 1550.

Richard Austen was born at Tenterden, Kent, England. He married Elizabeth Kenworthy.

They had four children: Robert Austen (1570), Margaret Austen (1573), John I Austen (1577) and William I Austen (1583). All of the children were born at Goudhurst, Kent, England, where their parents died, on the same day, 09 Feb 1620.

John I Austen married twice. His first wife was Margaret, and they had six children before she died about 1608.

He then re-married Katherine Bourne, our ancestor, in 1610, and they were blessed with five children.

Katherine Bourne was a direct descendant of King of England Edward I "Longshanks" Plantagenet

"Edward I is credited with many accomplishments during his reign, including restoring royal authority after the reign of Henry III, establishing parliament as a permanent institution and thereby also a functional system for raising taxes, and reforming the law through statutes.

At the same time, he is also often criticized for other actions, such as his brutal conduct towards the Scots, and issuing the Edict of Expulsion in 1290, by which the Jews were expelled from England.

The Edict remained in effect for the rest of the Middle Ages, and it would be over 350 years until it was formally overturned in 1656" – Wikipedia.

John died in 1620, at the age of forty two. That was the year his youngest twins were born.

His children with Margaret were: John II Austin (1601), Marie Austin (1603), Sara Austin (1604), Thomas Austin (1605), Alexander Austin (1606) and Elizabeth Austin (1607).

John and Katherine were the parents of: James I Austen (1611), Margaret Austen (1615), William Austen (1618), Joan and Lawrance Austen, the twins, were born the year their father died (1620).

James I Austen married a woman named Jane, and they had three sons: James II Austen (about 1641) , Thomas Austen (1643) Robert Austin (about 1650). James I Austen died in England, the year is unknown. Thomas died in Louisa, Virginia, date unknown. The only daughter was Rebecca Austen, (1647- 1717 New Kent, Virgina). She married Thomas Elmore.

Robert is the ancestor of Elvis Presley. Robert came to Amercia and married a Saponi Indian woman named Frances.

They were the parents of four children: John (1699), Richard (1700), Willam (1702) , and Lucy Austin (1705).

William married Ruth Bryant, and fathered three children: John, (1726), Charles (1727) and William Wilson Austin. (1730).

Charles Austin married Elizabeth McBee, the sister of Mary Mcbee who married John Champness II Austin, the son of John Champness I Austin and Hannah Love. Charles and Elizabeth are the fifth great grandparents of Elvis Presley.

James II Austen married Alice Waller, and their son was James III Austin (1669). James II Austin died about 1677 in Lamberhurst, Horsmoden, Kent, England.

James III Austen married Sarah. Her last name may have been Champness, but that is my own idea. That name appears for several generations to come. Their three sons were: Richard Austin (1695), Nathan Austin (1697) and John Champness I Austin (1701). The older sons were born in Marden, Kent, England, but John was born in Cornwall Kent England, according to his own statements.

James and Sarah both died in Kent, England, within a year of each other.

James died in 1700, before John was born, and Sarah died when John was a baby, in 1701. All three brothers emigrated to Lunenburg, Virginia, where they lived until their deaths.

Chapter Two

Our family story really begins with our first Austin ancestor in America. John Austin was born in the year 1701, in Kent England. John came to America about 1720.

John, we know, became Constable of Lunenburg County, Virginia in 1749 as stated in the book "Sunlight on the Southside", p 187, by L. Bell, a history of Lunenburg County.

He owned at least 1000 acres of land in the part of Lunenburg County, Virginia, which later became Charlotte, Halifax, and Pittsylvania counties, in Virginia.

John's wife was named Hannah Love. Researchers know that he also had a wife who was a Saponi Indian. Some researchers believe that they are the same woman, and that she was simply adopted into the Scottish/English family of Alexander Love and Elesha Basye.

As far as my own beliefs, personally, I agree with the that statement. It is very likely that, indeed, Hannah and the Indian woman, is the same woman. I also believe that Hannah was related to Frances, the Saponi woman who married Robert Austin, the great uncle of John Champness Austin. I believe that when John Champness Austin came to America with his brothers, he came to find his great uncle Robert.

Robert Austin had emigrated to America by 1698.

At any rate, John and his Indian wife had five known children: Richard Austin, John Austin Jr, Stephen Austin, Valentine Austin, and Joseph Austin. Mary Sally Austin and Hannah Austin are listed in some places as being daughters of John Austin.

Much of the Austin research has been done by many gifted researchers, and it is thoroughly documented by the Austin Family Association of America. In no way do I intend to infringe upon any of their research. I am simply writing our story down, so that our particular Austin line of descent will have a story, somewhat, of their heritage.

John Austin, Jr. identified himself as a Saponi Indian at a court hearing in Surry County. Valentine was also identified as an Indian at a court hearing in Surry County. Later, it was discovered the Richard and Joseph were identified by the state of Virginia as Melungeons (not of pure European blood).

Since four of the five known children have been identified as "mixed blood" it is felt that there was only one mother for all the known children." - Charles Edwin Austin- Austin researcher. All of the Austin sons married and became fathers of mostly large familes.

Valentine, Richard and Stephen moved to North Carolina, while our ancestor, John Austin Jr., along with Joseph, both stayed in Virginia. Although John Austin Jr did live briefly in Rowan County, North Carolina, around 1770, after the death of his father.

John Austin is listed under "Colonial Soldiers Lunenburg County Virginia" during the French and Indian Wars (1754-1763), in "The Old Free State," Vol. 1, p 195. Due to his age, this is more than likely John Austin Jr., since, according to records, was born in 1726.

John Austin Jr married Mary Susannah Crenshaw McBee-Magbee. She is the daughter of the William McBee, of Scottish descent, and his wife, Susannah Vardry, of English descent.

Some researchers firmly believe that Mary McBee was a Susquohanah Indian, based solely on the following information:

"INDIAN PEACE TREATY:

Found is a recording in the Rowan County (NC) Book, p 72 and dated 19 Apr 1755. Handwritten text was difficult to read (by Liz Austin Carlin), but best Effort follows.

TEXT: "Whereas John Auston (this would be John Austin, Jr.) and a Saponia Indian and Marry (Mary?) a Susquohanah Indian and Thomas Cattaba applied for a pass to the Catabe Nation being now on their journey to conclude a general peace with the Cattabas in behalf of the said nations and also presented three belts of Wampum to said Court by which the said Treaty is to be concluded."

I will let the reader decide if that is sufficient evidence for them. Mary could easily have been adopted by the McBee family. I simply do not have enough information to say for sure, either way. I do know the European heritage of William McBee and Susannah Vardry.

I also realize that the Mary mentioned in the Treaty could easily be any Mary.

At any rate, John Jr and Mary became the parents of six children, according to the data provided by other researchers.

They are: Stephen Austin, Isaiah Austin, William Austin, Joseph Austin, Thomas and John Austin, III. There are other researchers who also claim the children include: Elizabeth Austin, David Austin, Margaret Mary Austin and Hannah Austin.

Mary's sister, Elizabeth McBee, married a cousin of John Austin, one Charles Austin, also of Saponi descent.

Chapter Three

Stephen Austin is our ancestor. He was born 04 Nov 1755, in Pittsylvania, Virginia. Stephen enlisted in the Calvary of Maj. William Armstrong and Col. Washington in the light horse dragoons, in Gen. Greene's Division, in Surry County, North Carolina, when he was 21. He spent five years in the Revolutionary War, but the last two years hired a substitute.

In his pension application, Stephen states, that when he was about years of age, he was taken to Grayson County, Virginia.

The following is a copy of Stephen's pension letters:

November 4th, 1832   State of Tennessee Wayne County Circuit court of said county for the year 1832, November 4th.

On this 2nd day of November in A.D. 1832 personally appeared in open court before the judge of said court now sitting, Stephen Austin, a resident of said County, aged seventy-seven years and five months, who first being duly sworn according to law, doth on his oath make the following declaration, in order to obtain the benefit of the Act of Congress - pertaining -7th 1832.

I had entered the service of the United States - that is to say- He listed and went into the Continental service in the county of Surry and state of North Carolina, for the whole term of the war.

He marched through North Carolina, into South Carolina on as far --------------? six? by the Hanging Rock, Camden and was at the Cowpans (sp.) (Cowpens), but not in the Battle fought at that place.

He was marched through South Carolina- He was in hearing of the Battle at Guilford (courthouse) in North Carolina in Guilford (?) county. He belonged to the light horses and was posted outside the lines to guard the flank.

He was in a great many skirmishes, but no regular engagements. His principal service being provided in guarding and surveying the country and protecting foraging parties.

He was in actual service during the Revolutionary was five years - and hired a substitute for the last two years of the war - who served for that period in the place of the applicant.

He was in Virginia, also in the service of the United States some part of the time of his service.

(page 2)

He entered upon the service at about the age of twenty one years under under the command of Captain William Armstrong who was afterwards promoted to the place of Major of the Calvary - and Col. Washington of the light horse dragoons, in General Green's division.

He knew General (?) Senter and General Rutherford (?) and General Locke (?) The above is a statement of all the service which application states he positively did perform, and was honorably discharged. His said discharge has long since been destroyed. He has no documentary evidence and he knows of no person whose testimony he can procure, who can testify to his service. He hereby relinquishes every claim whatever to a pension or ----?-----?------, and declares that his name is not on the Pension Role (?) of the Agency of any state.

-Stephen Austin-

(signed with his mark)

After the war Stephen went back to Virginia and lived there 20 years. He moved to Tennessee and lived in Warren, Giles, Wayne and Hardin Counties, and he also lived in Alabama for three years.

Family tradition among the descendants of Stephen would seem to indicate that he was sort of a "wagon master" who made trips back to North Carolina and Virginia, and led settlers from there into Tennessee.

As is the habit of several of his descendants: Stephen refused to settle down for long. Supposedly, he made his last trip when he was 70 years old and came back with 30 families, mostly relatives from Virginia and North Carolina.

They settled in Wayne County, Tennessee, along Second Creek, in Hardin County, Tennessee along Holland's Creek, and Lauderdale County, Alabama, along Bumpas' Creek.

Since he does not show up in many census schedules, this seems like a likely explanation for these absences.

Stephen "Baldy" Austin died in Hardin County, Tennessee, at the age of 88. He had lived a long and productive life, by all accounts. He married Dorcas Pinson, who was born in 1756, also from Virginia. Together, they had successfully raised a family of twelve children. They are both buried at Holland's Creek Cemetery in Hardin, Tennessee.

I was privileged several years ago, to visit Holland's Creek Cemetery with my father. I always wished that we could go back again: sadly that was not to be.

I will always be grateful for the time that we did get to visit it together.

Here is a photo of Stephen's gravesite:

I must include here that Dorcas Pinson, daughter of Judge Aaron Pinson Jr and Delila Stovall, is of Swedish ancestry. Her father was blind at the time his will was written in 1801. He signed it with his mark.

"The Reverend Aaron Pinson was a frontiersman. He served in the militia during the French and Indian War. He was one of the first Baptist ministers in the Carolinas and was appointed Judge by the Continental Congress in the area of what is now Northwestern Tennessee, but at the time was on the edege of the frontier. He constantly traveled around great events and great historic figures. He was a peer of the great Indian fighter, Sevier, who became the first governor of Tennessee, and of Selby, the first governor of Kentucky. He almost certainly knew Daniel Boone and also Davy Crocket's grandparents. He was an intimate of Sterns and Marshall who are famous for founding the Baptist church in the South." - Ancestry.com

Dorcas' paternal grandmother was Elizabeth Rambo (Swedish ancestry). Her grandfather was Aaron Pinson, Sr.

One Ricardo Pinzon, printer, went from his native Spain to England before 1476.

He owned and operated a printing shop on Fleet Street, London.

It was said that he was an Uncle of the three Pinsons that sailed with Columbus.

From a manuscript, PINSON, by Leonardo Andres:

"Three Spanish brothers sailed from Palos with Christopher Columbus.- Capt. Martin Alonso Pinzon owned the ship Pinta and commanded that ship in the Columbus expedition, while his brother Francisco Pinzon was the pilot on the Pinta. The younger of the three brothers, Capt. Vincento Yanes Pinzon, commanded the ship Nina.

Later on the sons of these three brothers were employed as navigators by the Spainish, Portugese, French, and English governments. Some settled in the various countries.

Other and younger family members of these three took up large land grants in the Spainish provinces of Cuba, Texas, Mexico, and Florida and the surname is still numerous in these lands. Of the Pinzons who migrated to England came the Pinsons of Virginia."

Aaron's ancestor was none other than Captain Martin Alonso Pinzon., who owned the Nina and the Pinta, with his brothers.

He sailed the Pinta, while his brother, Vicente Yanez Pinzon sailed the Nina. Neither wanted to sail Columbus' boats, unsure of the abilities of the boats. There is much to be read online about the Pinzon brothers, and, I am still trying to prove defininitevly which brother is our ancestor. I believe Martin is probable, but there seems to be a lack of information on his actual descendants.

Back to Aaron Pinson, Sr.

"Note: William Byrd, while exploring the backwoods of Virginia in 1730 found Aaron living on Tewahominy Creek, a stream now on the dividing line between Halifax and Mecklenburg counties.

Byrd noted in his journal that Pinson was the settler farthest West in the area and he renamed the stream Aaron's Creek which it bears today. Aaron Pinson is traditionally the first settler of Halifax Co. Virginia."

Dorcas' third great grandfather was none other than Peter Gunnarson Rambo (1612-1698).

Peter Gunnarson Rambo was a Swedish immigrant to New Sweden who lived as a farmer and served as a justice on the Governor's Council.

Peter Gunnarson Rambo was the longest living of the original settlers and became known as the Father of New Sweden.

At the age of twenty-seven, Peter Gunnersson sailed to New Sweden as a laborer on the second voyage of the Kalmar Nyckel in 1639-40, the first voyage in which permanent settlers were aboard. Upon arrival he took on the name Rambo.

It is speculated that the name Rambo was derived from a shortened form of "Ramberget" plus "bo".

Ramberget (or "Raven Mountain") is located on the island of Hisingen, which today is part of Gothenburg. Translation of "bo" from Swedish to English is "resident" or "nest".

It is known that Peter Gunnarsson lived in or near Gothenburg before leaving for New Sweden, and in Gunnarsson's time, the island of Hisingen was mostly farmland.

It is not known whether or not Peter Gunnarsson came to New Sweden voluntarily.

He was indentured by the company to plant tobacco on the New Sweden Company's plantation just outside the fort. He become a freeman, and by 1644, he was growing tobacco for the New Sweden Trading Company.

Rambo's Rock along the Schuylkill River is named for his family.

Peter Gunnarsson married Brita Mattsdotter (her father being Matt .... hence she was Matts' daughter).

They had five children: Peter II, Gunnar, John, Andreas, Gertrude and Katherine.

Peter Kalm, a Swede who traveled in North America between 1748 and 1751, wrote in his diary about his interview with Mr. Peter Rambo, grandson of Peter Gunnarsson Rambo.

Peter Rambo, the younger, told him that his grandfather "had brought apple seeds and several other tree and garden seeds with him in a box."

The first Rambo apple tree may have been produced from one of these seeds.

William Coxe's "A View of the Cultivation of Fruit Trees, and the Management of Orchards and Cider", published in 1817, indicates that the Rambo apple was much cultivated in Delaware, Pennsylvania, and New Jersey and took "its name from the families by whom it was introduced into notice."

The Rambo is confused with but is not closely related to the Summer Rambo. Because of the confusion, the Rambo has also been called the Winter Rambo.

Now, back to the Austin Family. Dorcas and Stephen Austin were the parents of: Josiah Austin, William Austin, Saunders Austin, Robert Austin, Benjamin and Elizabeth Austin, who were twins, John Austin, Stephen Austin, Jr., Rebecca Austin, Richard Austin, Hannah Austin, and, Ransom Austin. All of the children were born in Virginia.

Three of them died in Hardin County, Tennessee, one of which was our ancestor, Saunders Austin, along with Elizabeth and Benjamin.

Three more of them, Josiah, William and Rebecca, all died in Illinois. Robert and John seemed to have stayed in Alabama: Hannah and Ransom went to Arkansas.

Chapter Four

Saunders Austin was born in 1782, Grayson, Montgomery, Virginia. He came to Tennessee with his father, and married Nancy Qualls, who was born in 1790, in the Qualla Cherokee Nation North Carolina. Nancy was of Indian descent, her third great grandmother was Jane Tunstall, the daughter of Marshall Tunstall and Jane Fox. Jane's brother, Thomas, married Mary Tunstall, the sister of Marshall Tunstall.

Jane was the grand daughter of Unity Ursala Croshaw, whose grandmother was Ursula Unity Patawomeck, the daughter of Japasaw Oppasus The Great Chief Patawomeke Powhatan, and probably a asister of Wahunsenacawh Powhatan (the father of Matoaka Amonute Pocahontas Powhatan).

Ursala Patawomeke married Raleigh Croshaw, an Englishman who immigrated to Virgiina and left his English wife at home. He supposedly named his Indian wife with the same name of his English wife, Ursala Daniels Croshaw.

When his English wife came to Virgiina and discovered his new family, she was not very happy. She left him to live with his new family.

Nancy and Saunders were married in 1806, in Warren, Tennessee.

They moved to Hardin County and raised a family of eleven children. Saunders is buried at Holland's Creek Cemetery, Hardin, Tennessee, and so is Nancy.

Their children are: Stephen Bally Austin, Elizabeth Austin, Mary Austin, John Bally Austin, James J. Austin, David Austin, William (Dock) Austin, Angeline Austin, Archibald Sanders Austin, Robert Austin, and Enoch Austin.

All but one, possibly two, of the children remained in Hardin, Tennessee their entire lives. Below is a photo that I created from three separate photos of three of the brothers:

Sons of Saunders Stephen & Nancy Qualls Austin

Stephen Bally 1809-1872   John Bally 1816-1896   Archibald Sanders 1826

All of the children married and became parents to several children of their own.

Stephen Bally Austin, Mary Austin, John Bally Austin and Enoch Austin, all married into the Lamb family. They all married siblings except for Enoch, who married their niece, Elizabeth Lamb. The spouses were of Shawnee descent through their mother, Mary Sallie Goodman. Their father was Archibald III Lamb.

John Bally Austin had a second wife of the Qualls family, as did William (Dock) Austin, Angeline Austin, Archibald Sanders Austin (he was married three times). William (Dock) Austin and Angeline Austin married siblings, children of John D. Qualls and Mary Lamb.

Chapter Five

Stephen Bally Austin married Anna (Annie) Lamb, who was born in 1813, to Archibald Henry II Lamb and Mary Sallie Goodman. They were married in Tennessee, 1829.

One local researcher, Mac Lambert, states that Stephen was a school teacher in Hardin County. Stephen and Anna lived there and raised a family of twelve children.

Annie Lamb's mother, Mary Sallie Goodman, was the seventh great granddaughter of Cheif Ensenore Powhatan and the sixth great granddaughter of Japasaw Oppasus The Great Chief of the Patawomeke. Japasaw married the daughter of Cheif Ensenore Powhatan. She was a distant cousin of Jane Fox, wife of Marshall Tunstall.

The families did tend to stay together through marriages. It was a common practice among Indan relations.

Mary Sallie Goodman's ancestor was Ursula Unity Patawomeck, who married a colonist, Raleigh Croshaw.

There is much evidence to prove this fact, though many doubt it: simply because Croshaw did have an English wife. Her name happened to be Ursala Daniels Croshaw. Raleigh Croshaw, supposedly, for some reason, called his Indian wife by that name, also.

His English wife was not in America at the time his children were born. She had stayed in England: proving that our ancestor, unquestionably, had to be his Indian wife. Ursala Daniels Croshaw came to Virginia on the "Bona Nova" in 1620, years after his first children with our Ursala were born. She died in either 1624 or 1625, in York Virginia. Her unhappiness over her husband's new family was probably profound.

In 1622, Croshaw's father-in-law, Japasaw, refused the order of his half-brother Opechan Stream-Powhatan , (or, as he is known, Opechancanough) to kill the "husband of his daughter: Raleigh Croshaw".   This act led to the Patawomeck people withdrawing from the Powhatan Confederacy.

"NARRATIVES OF EARLY VIRGINIA   1622 vourers and opposers, with their arguments (pro) and (con) would bee too tedious and needlesse being so publukely knowne ; the which to estabhsh, spent a good part of that yeere, and the beginning of the next. This made many thinke wonders of Virginia, to pay such pensions extraordinary to a few here that were never there, and also in what state and pompe some Chieftaines and divers of their associates live in Virginia ; and yet no money to maintaine a Garrison, pay poore men their wages, nor yet five and twenty pence to all the Adventurers here, and very little to the most part of the Planters there, bred such differences in opinion it was dissolved. Now let us returne to Captaine Croshaw at Patawomek, where he had not beene long ere Opechancanough sent two baskets of beads to this King, to kill him and his man, assuring him of the Massacre he had made, and that before the end of two Moones there should not be an Enghshman in all their Countries : "

"this fearefull message the King (Chief Japasaw) told this Captaine (Croshaw), who replied, he had seene both the cowardise and trechery of Opechancanough sufficiently tried by Captaine Smith, therefore liis threats he feared not, nor for his favour cared, but would nakedly fight with him or any of his with their owne swords; if he were slaine, he would leave a letter for his Country men to know, the fault was his owne, not the Kings.

Two dayes the King(Chief Japasaw) deliberated upon an answer, at last told him the Engish were his friends, and the Salvage Emperour Opitchapam, now called Toyatan, was his brother; therefore there should be no bloud shed betwixt them : for hee returned the Presents, willing the Pamaunkes to come no more in his Country, lest the English, though against his will, should doe them any mischief.

Not long after, a Boat going abroad to seeke out some releefe amongst the Plantations, by Nuports-newes met such ill weather, though the men were saved they lost their boat, which the storme and waves cast upon the shore of Nandsamund : where Edward Waters one of the three that first stayed. The charter. At Pamuiikey in 1609."

Ursala Unity Patawomeck, to narrow it down for my readers, was probably the first cousin of Matoaka Amonute Powhatan, or Pocahontas. Her mother was proabably the sister of Pocahontas' father, Wahunsenacawh Powhatan.

The children of Annie Lamb and Stephen Austin were: Rachel Austin (who married a cousin, Archibald Qualls), Mary Dolly Ann Austin (who married James C. Milligan), Henry Lamb Austin (who married Mary Elizabeth Hardwick), Benjamin H. Austin (who married a cousin, Mary Polly Austin), John T. Austin, Nancy Austin (who married William Wiley Mangum), Martha Jane Austin (who also married a cousin, Henry Lamb).

Archibald Austin (who also married twice; once to his cousin, Mary "Polly" Austin, then to Matilda "Tilda" Shelby), Sarah Elizabeth "Babe" Austin (who married a distant cousin, Robert Bobgate H A Qualls), Louisa Lou Austin (who married twice; once to Zebulon Sharp, then to Samuel Stricklin), Enoch B. Austin (who married a cousin, Sarah M. Rebecca Cossey) and Sanders M Austin (who also married a cousin, Nancy Ann Qualls).

Chapter Six

Rachel Austin was born 29 Dec 1830, in Hardin County. She lived there her entire life, marrying a cousin, Archibald Qualls. She died in 1928, he died in 1887.

They had nine children: Mary A Qualls, Sarah E Qualls, Louisa E Qualls, Julia Qualls, Nipsy M Qualls, John Qualls, Martha Flora Qualls, Francis Qualls, and Stephen H. Qualls. All of them stayed in Hardin County, as well.

Mary Dolly Ann Austin was born 07 Sep 1834 in Hardin County. She married James C. Milligan, and they also stayed in Hardin County. She died in 1918, he died in 1875.

They had six children: Lucinda Milligan, Nancy Ann Milligan, Martha Elizabeth Milligan, Sarah Matilda Milligan, Stephen Aranamous Milligan and Enoch Milligan, all of whom stayed in Hardin County.

Henry Lamb Austin was born 11 Nov 1835, in Hardin County. He married Mary Elizabeth Hardwick, They left Tennessee and moved west, to Shawnee, Pottawatomie, Oklahoma, after their children were born.

All of the children went with them, so they may have moved when the children were small. They both died in 1919.

They had thirteen children:

Stephen Conrad Austin, Benjamin M. Austin, Martha Lucinda Austin, Mary Ann Austin, Morgan Austin (Morgan and Mary Ann both died very young: he was eleven, she was seventeen) William Charles A Austin, Sarah Louise Austin, Isadora Dora Austin, Rachel Susannah Lavanah/LouAnna Austin,Henry Cornelieus Austin, Robin Luther Austin, Enoch Wheeler Austin, and Eli Hugh Austin.

Enoch Wheeler Austin was the inventor of the "split wheel rim'" (1926) for the tubeless tire, used in WWII, and on many vehicles/jeeps during the war.

The wheel was used after the war but no financial compensation was ever offered by the government or sub-contractors so Enoch Wheeler Austin began legal proceedings. Willys Jeep, and Ford, made/used the wheels.

Sadly, Enoch died before anything could be filed, or settled. There are four other patented inventions of his on file at Washington DC.

(This history is from Henry David Austin...son...and grandson, Jerry M Tillison: and it is on file at the U.S. Patent Office, in Washington, D.C.)

Benjamin H. Austin was born in 1837, in Hardin County. He married a cousin, Mary Polly Austin, and they stayed in Hardin County. He died in 1904: she died in 1911.

They had ten children: Rachel Matilda Austin, Thomas Frank Austin, William Owen Austin, Martha Mattie Austin, Timothy J Austin, Minnie Austin, Mary C Austin, Frinetly Austin, Arthur Garfield Austin and Gertrude Leona Austin.

The family stayed in Hardin, Tennessee.

John T Austin was born in 1840, in Hardin County. Most researchers believe that he only had one wife, Sarah Armstrong. During my research, I recieved a copy of the death record of his son, Henry, that clearly states his mother was Eliza Qualls.

I believe that she was, in fact, Elizabeth Qualls, daughter of Gatewood and Mildred Bouldin Qualls. She obvciously died young, possibly even in childbirth. Henry was born in 1860 and she was dead by 1864. John had married Sarah in 1865, when Henry was only five. The reason I beleive she is a daughter of Gatewood and Mildred Bouldin Qualls is simple. Knowing how families did stay together and often married siblings: her sister and brother both married John's siblings.

Henry Austin, son of John T Austin, was born 07 Aug 1860 Hardin County.

John married Sarah, and they had Lucinda C Austin, Soloman A. Austin, James T Austin and Stephen Alfred Austin. John T Austin died in 1913, and Sarah died in 1912.

Nancy Austin, daughter of Stephen Bally Austin and Annie Lamb, was born in 1842 in Hardin County. She married William Wiley Mangum. She died in 1885, and he died in 1922, in Hardin County.

They had five children: Pressley C. Mangum (who also ended up in Oklahoma Territory), Wiley Daniel Mangum, Stephen Howell Mangum (he died in Marlow, Stephens, Oklahoma), Lucy Mangum and Mattie Martha Mangum.

Martha Jane Austin was born 11 Mar 1844 in Hardin County. She married a cousin, Henry II Lamb. She died in 1895, he died in 1929, both in Hardin County.

I only have record of four children, all dying at birth.

Archibald Austin was born in 1845, in Hardin County. He married twice. His first wife was his cousin, Mary "Polly" Austin. She was the daughter of William (Dock) Austin. She died in 1901, after having eleven children with Arch.

They were: John Carroll Austin, Sarah Ann Austin, Martha A. Austin, William Otis Austin, Stephen Walker Austin, Ira Lewis Austin, Owen Austin, Waymon Reece Austin, (con't next page)

Archibald Savage Austin, Mary Birdie Austin and Tiger R. Austin. Arch then remarried a woman named Matilda "Tilda" Shelby and they had two daughters: Flossy Edith Austin and Fleety Ethel Austin.

Fleety only lived 3 months. Arch died in 1914, and Tilly died in 1935, both in Hardin County.

Sarah Elizabeth "Babe" Austin was born in 1848, in Hardin, Tennessee. She married a distant cousin, Robert Bobgate H A Qualls. They had at least six children born in Hardin County, before moving to Stephens, Marlow, Oklahoma. Their children were: Stephen J. Qualls, James Wiley Qualls, John Robert Gate Qualls, William Caroll Qualls, Matt Franklin Qualls and Millie Ann Qualls.

Robert L Qualls, Romdes Qualls and Stella Qualls were born later, and I cannot be sure where they were born.

Babe Austin Qualls died in 1929, as did her husband.

Louisa Lou Austin was born in 1851, in Hardin County. She married Zebulon Sharp. They had six children: Henry Sharp, Martha Jane Sharp, Della Sharp, John William Loyd Sharp, Annie Lee Sharp and Clint Martin Sharp. They all lived in Hardin County. Zeb died in 1929, Waterloo, Lauderdale, Alabama, where they had lived for a while.

Lou Austin remarried Samuel Stricklin, and she died in Hardin County after 1930.

Enoch B. Austin was born in 1858, Hardin County. He married a cousin, Sarah M. Rebecca Cossey.

They had two children: Idah Belle Austin, and Estillee Austin. I do not know Enoch's death date.

Sanders M Austin was born in 1832, Hardin County. Sanders married a cousin, Nancy Ann Qualls. He died in 1931, in Hardin County.

Chapter Seven

Henry Austin was the son of John T Austin and Eliza (Elizabeth) Qualls. Henry was born 07 Aug 1860 in Hardin County, Tennessee and died 16 Feb 1947, in Alcorn County Mississippi. According to his death record, on file with McPeters' Funeral Home, he died of hypertensive apoplexy ... possibly a stroke.

Henry married Rosa Elizabeth Britnell, a relative of the Cherokee Proctor family. From her son's death certificate, I believe her maiden name was Terrell, but her stepfather, John Wesley Campbell Britnell, raised her.

She had four children from a previous marriage to George Washington Raines: John William "Will" Raines, Docia/Dotia Bell Raines, Mollie Louise Raines and Minnie M Raines. Will was nineteen when his mother married Henry: the girls were younger.

Henry and Rosa had four more children: George Edward "Edd" Austin (1900 Hardin, Tennessee-1953 Paragould, Greene, Arkansas) James Alfred Austin (1902 Hardin, Tennessee-1988 Leachville, Mississippi, Arkansas) Ernest Rowden Austin (1904 Hardin, Tennessee-1995 St Charles, Missouri) (con't next page) and Carlie Pearl Austin (1905 Hardin, Tennessee-1973 Alcorn, Mississippi).

   After Rosa's death in 1918, Henry remarried Oley Parrish.

   Here is a photo that I created, of Rosa, with five of her eight children.   L-R back are: Alfred and Carlie Austin, with Will Raines. In front, L-R, are Edd Austin and Mollie Raines .

Edd married Mary Alice Sagely when he was about 20, and had two children. They divorced and he moved to Arkansas, where his brother Will, had already moved. Edd remarried Pearl Evaline Yancey in 1928, and they had nine children, three of whom lived to be adults. Pearl died in 1941.

Edd married a woman named Jennie shorly after Pearl's death. That marriage didn't last long.

Edd then re-married a widow, Bessie Lee Louise Draffen Remagen. He was killed in 1953 by a falling tree, while working on Hurricane Ditch, east of Marmaduke, Arkansas.

James Alfred Austin married Willie May Hatley, and they had five children, four of whom lived to be adults. They moved to Arkansas, near where his brothers were.

Ernest Rowden Austin also moved to Arkansas, where he married a widow, Viola Berry Kuykendall. She was the mother of Royce Kendall, father in the country music duo, with his daughter, Jeannie: the Kendall's.

Royce had a brother, Floyce, who died in 2003. Royce and Floyce were known very early as the Austin Brothers.

Carlie Pearl Austin married Elcy Kilpatrick, and they had one son and adopted a daughter.

Many are the stories of our ancestors: it is up to us to tell them, again and again.

It is up to us, and to our children, to pass these stories along. For the days of long ago will live again, through our stories. Our ancestors will live again, as we tell of their lives, and their successes: even their failures. For without them, none of us would be here today.

I hope that all of my readers will treasure their heritage, and proudly pass it down to future generations.

"Generations pass like leaves fall from our family tree. Each season new life blossoms and grows benefiting from the strength and experience of those who went before." -Heidi Swapp

"We are Austin's, we will not be forgotten!"

I leave you with a poem that I received many years ago. Author unknown, it is simply titled "The Storytellers":

"We are the chosen. My feelings are in each family there is one who seems called to find the ancestors.

To put flesh on their bones and make them live again, to tell the family story and to feel that somehow they know and approve.

To me, doing genealogy is not a cold gathering of facts but, instead, breathing life into all who have gone before.

We are the story tellers of the tribe. All tribes have one. We have been called as it were by our genes.

Those who have gone before cry out to us: Tell our story. So, we do.

In finding them, we somehow find ourselves. How many graves have I stood before now and cried? I have lost count.

How many times have I told the ancestors you have a wonderful family and you would be proud of us?

How many times have I walked up to a grave and felt somehow there was love there for me? I cannot say.

It goes beyond just documenting facts. It goes to who am I and why do I do the things I do? It goes to seeing a cemetery about to be lost forever to weeds and indifference and saying I can't let this happen. The bones here are bones of my bone and flesh of my flesh. It goes to doing something about it.

It goes to pride in what our ancestors were able to accomplish. How they contributed to what we are today. It goes to respecting their hardships and losses, their never giving in or giving up, their resoluteness to go on and build a life for their family."

"It goes to deep pride that they fought to make and keep us a Nation. It goes to a deep and immense understanding that they were doing it for us.

That we might be born who we are. That we might remember them. So we do. With love and caring and scribing each fact of their existence, because we are them and they are us.

So, as a scribe called, I tell the story of my family. It is up to that one called in the next generation to answer the call and take their place in the long line of family storytellers.

That, is why I do my family genealogy, and that is what calls those young and old to step up and put flesh on the bones."

About the author:

Wanda Austin Nelson is an Indie author who was born and raised in the beautiful southern state of Mississippi. She traveled with her parents to the Ozarks in Arkansas many times. Living near the Civil War battle grounds of Shiloh, in Tennessee, she is well grounded in history. Family stories fascinated her. Those experiences created in her a strong desire to travel and learn about her ancestors.

After researching her family for over twenty years, she wrote some of it in a family history/cookbook, and later added a series of genealogy books: Our Family Genealogy.

Mrs. Nelson is a devout Christian, and that commitment led to writing two inspirational/devotional books.

The Land of lost Socks is her first children's book, written in honor of her nieces and nephews.

She lives in Colorado, with her family. Taking long walks with her husband is one of her favorite activities, when she isn't writing or spending time with her family.

Mrs. Nelson is a member of Goodreads, and Christian Indie Authors.

Author interview: http://awesomegang.com/wanda-austin-nelson/

http://www.wandaaustinnelson.com/

http://www.amazon.com/Wanda-Nelson

If you have enjoyed this book, please let Mrs. Nelson know! She would love to hear from you!

WandaNelson.author@gmail.com

Other books by Mrs. Nelson:

*God's Peace Pact

*Our Family Genealogy - the Austin Family (Volume 1)

*Our Family Genealogy - the Bragg Family (Volume 2)

*Our Family Genealogy - the Yancey Family (Volume 3)

*Our Family Genealogy - the Perkins Family (Volume 4)

*Our Family Genealogy - the Langston Family (Volume 5)

*Our Family Genealogy - the Qualls/Quarles Family (Volume 6)

*Our Family Genealogy - the Prince Family (Volume 7)

*Our Family Genealogy - the Wingo Family (Volume 8)

*Tracks of my Father: Joe's Story

*Land of Lost Socks

*State of Grace

 *Yancey Family: Timeless Treasures: Stories and Recipes

Made in the USA
Coppell, TX
11 December 2022

88659334R00036